Great Literature Copywork

Practice Handwriting with Excerpts from the Great Books

Classic Copywork Vol. 1

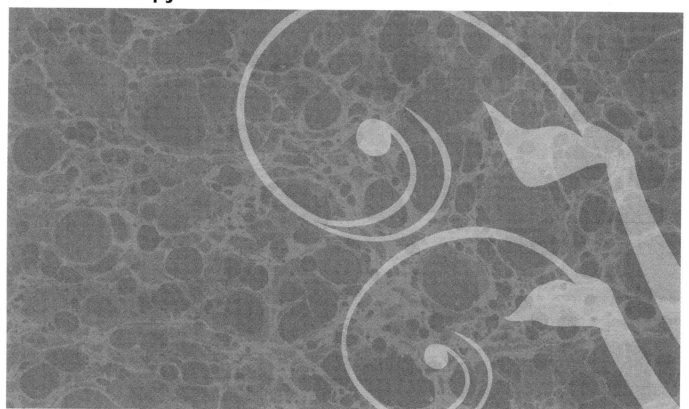

Copyright © 2014 Ruth Lestina
All rights reserved.

ISBN: 061595457X
ISBN-13: 978-0615954578

Table of Contents

Robert Frost: The Road Not Taken

Two roads diverged in a yellow wood,
And sorry I could not travel both
And be one traveler, long I stood
And looked down one as far as I could
To where it bent in the undergrowth;

Then took the other, as just as fair,
And having perhaps the better claim,
Because it was grassy and wanted wear;
Though as for that the passing there
Had worn them really about the same,

And both that morning equally lay
In leaves no step had trodden black.
Oh, I kept the first for another day!
Yet knowing how way leads on to way,
I doubted if I should ever come back.

I shall be telling this with a sigh
Somewhere ages and ages hence:
Two roads diverged in a wood, and I
I took the one less traveled by,
And that has made all the difference.

Two roads diverged in a yellow wood,

And sorry I could not travel both

And be one traveler, long I stood

And looked down one as far as I could

To where it bent in the undergrowth;

Then took the other, as just as fair,

And having perhaps the better claim,

Because it was grassy and wanted wear;

Though as for that the passing there

Had worn them really about the same,

And both that morning equally lay

In leaves no step had trodden black.

Oh, I kept the first for another day!

Yet knowing how way leads on to way,

I doubted if I should ever come back.

I shall be telling this with a sigh

Somewhere ages and ages hence:

Two roads diverged in a wood, and I

I took the one less traveled by,

And that has made all the difference.

The Road Not Taken by Robert Frost

Shakespeare: Julius Caesar, Act 1 Scene 2

Why, man, he doth bestride the narrow world
Like a Colossus; and we petty men
Walk under his huge legs, and peep about
To find ourselves dishonourable graves.
Men at some time are masters of their fates:
The fault, dear Brutus, is not in our stars,
But in ourselves, that we are underlings.

Why, man, he doth bestride the narrow world

Like a Colossus; and we petty men

Walk under his huge legs, and peep about

To find ourselves dishonourable graves.

Men at some time are masters of their fates:

The fault, dear Brutus, is not in our stars,

But in ourselves, that we are underlings.

Shakespeare, "Julius Caesar", Act 1 Scene 2

Edgar Allen Poe: The Raven

Once upon a midnight dreary,
while I pondered, weak and weary,
Over many a quaint and curious
volume of forgotten lore —

While I nodded, nearly napping,
suddenly there came a tapping,
As of some one gently rapping,
rapping at my chamber door.

"'Tis some visiter," I muttered,
"tapping at my chamber door--
Only this and nothing more."

Once upon a midnight dreary, while I pondered,

weak and weary, Over many a quaint and curious

volume of forgotten lore-- While I nodded,

nearly napping, suddenly there came a tapping,

As of some one gently rapping, rapping at

my chamber door. "'Tis some visiter," I muttered,

"tapping at my chamber door--

Only this and nothing more".

The Raven by Edgar Allen Poe

David Brendan Hopes: A Sense of the Morning

If I love nature, it is not because nature is beautiful -- though, of course, it is beautiful -- but because it bears witness. The witness it bears is terrible and uncompromising.

If I love nature, it is not because nature is

beautiful -- though, of course, it is beautiful -- but

because it bears witness. The witness it bears is

terrible and uncompromising.

A Sense of the Morning by David Brendan Hopes

Aristotle: Metaphysics

Those who assert that the mathematical sciences say nothing of the beautiful or the good are in error. For these sciences say and prove a great deal about them; if they do not expressly mention them, but prove attributes which are their results or definitions, it is not true that they tell us nothing about them. The chief forms of beauty are order and symmetry and definiteness, which the mathematical sciences demonstrate in a special degree.

Those who assert that the mathematical sciences say

nothing of the beautiful or the good are in error.

For these sciences say and prove a great deal

about them; if they do not expressly mention

them, but prove attributes which are their

results or definitions, it is not true that they

tell us nothing about them. The chief forms

of beauty are order and symmetry and

definiteness, which the mathematical sciences

demonstrate in a special degree.

Metaphysics by Aristotle

Shakespeare: Julius Caesar, Act 3 Scene 1

I could be well moved, if I were as you:
If I could pray to move, prayers would move me:
But I am constant as the northern star,
Of whose true-fix'd and resting quality
There is no fellow in the firmament.
The skies are painted with unnumber'd sparks,
They are all fire and every one doth shine,
But there's but one in all doth hold his place:
So in the world; 'tis furnish'd well with men,
And men are flesh and blood, and apprehensive;
Yet in the number I do know but one

I could be well moved, if I were as you:

If I could pray to move, prayers would move me:

But I am constant as the northern star,

Of whose true-fix'd and resting quality

There is no fellow in the firmament.

The skies are painted with unnumber'd sparks,

They are all fire and every one doth shine,

But there's but one in all doth hold his place:

So in the world; 'tis furnish'd well with men,

And men are flesh and blood, and apprehensive;

Yet in the number I do know but one

Julius Caesar, Act 1 Scene 2, by Shakespeare

Charles Dickens: A Tale of Two Cities

It was the best of times, it was the worst of times,
it was the age of wisdom, it was the age of foolishness,
it was the epoch of belief, it was the epoch of incredulity,
it was the season of Light, it was the season of Darkness,
it was the spring of hope, it was the winter of despair,
we had everything before us, we had nothing before us,
we were all going direct to Heaven, we were all going direct the other way-
in short, the period was so far like the present period,
that some of its noisiest authorities insisted on its being received,
for good or for evil, in the superlative degree of comparison only.

It was the best of times, it was the worst of times,

it was the age of wisdom, it was the age of foolishness

it was the epoch of belief, it was the epoch of incredulity,

it was the season of Light, it was the season of

Darkness, it was the spring of hope, it was the winter

of despair, we had everything before us, we had nothing

before us, we were all going direct to Heaven, we were

all going direct the other way; in short, the period was

so far like the present period, that some of its noisiest

authorities insisted on its being received, for good or for

evil, in the superlative degree of comparison only.

A Tale of Two Cities by Charles Dickens

Frank Herbert: Dune

I must not fear. Fear is the mind-killer. Fear is the little-death that brings total obliteration. I will face my fear. I will permit it to pass over me and through me. And when it has gone past I will turn the inner eye to see its path. Where the fear has gone there will be nothing. Only I will remain.

I must not fear. Fear is the mind-killer.

Fear is the little-death that brings total

obliteration. I will face my fear. I will permit it

to pass over me and through me. And when it has

gone past I will turn the inner eye to see its path.

Where the fear has gone there will be nothing.

Only I will remain.

Dune by Frank Herbert

Abraham Lincoln: Gettysburg Address

Four score and seven years ago our fathers brought forth on this continent, a new nation, conceived in Liberty, and dedicated to the proposition that all men are created equal. Now we are engaged in a great civil war, testing whether that nation or any nation so conceived and so dedicated, can long endure. We are met on a great battle-field of that war. We have come to dedicate a portion of that field, as a final resting place for those who here gave their lives that that nation might live. It is altogether fitting and proper that we should do this.

But, in a larger sense, we can not dedicate -- we can not consecrate -- we can not hallow -- this ground. The brave men, living and dead, who struggled here, have consecrated it, far above our poor power to add or detract. The world will little note, nor long remember what we say here, but it can never forget what they did here. It is for us the living, rather, to be dedicated here to the unfinished work which they who fought here have thus far so nobly advanced. It is rather for us to be here dedicated to the great task remaining before us -- that from these honored dead we take increased devotion to that cause for which they gave the last full measure of devotion -- that we here highly resolve that these dead shall not have died in vain -- that this nation, under God, shall have a new birth of freedom -- and that government of the people, by the people, for the people, shall not perish from the earth.

Four score and seven years ago our fathers brought

forth on this continent, a new nation, conceived

in Liberty, and dedicated to the proposition that all

men are created equal. Now we are engaged in a

great civil war, testing whether that nation or any

nation so conceived and so dedicated, can long

endure. We are met on a great battle-field of that

war. We have come to dedicate a portion of that

field, as a final resting place for those who here gave

their lives that that nation might live. It is

altogether fitting and proper that we should do this.

But, in a larger sense, we can not dedicate -- we

can not consecrate -- we can not hallow -- this

ground. The brave men, living and dead, who

struggled here, have consecrated it, far above our

poor power to add or detract. The world will little

note, nor long remember what we say here, but it

can never forget what they did here. It is for us the

living, rather, to be dedicated here to the unfinished

work which they who fought here have thus far so

nobly advanced. It is rather for us to be here

dedicated to the great task remaining

before us -- that from these honored dead we take

increased devotion to that cause for which they gave

the last full measure of devotion -- that we here

highly resolve that these dead shall not have died in

vain -- that this nation, under God, shall have a

new birth of freedom -- and that government of the

people, by the people, for the people, shall not perish

from the earth.

Gettysburg. Address. by. Abraham. Lincoln.

Tad Williams: The Green Angel Tower

*We tell lies when we are afraid...
afraid of what we don't know, afraid of
what others will think, afraid of what
will be found out about us. But every
time we tell a lie, the thing that we fear
grows stronger.*

We tell lies when we are afraid...

afraid of what we don't know, afraid of

what others will think, afraid of what

will be found out about us. But every

time we tell a lie, the thing that we fear

grows stronger.

To Green Angel Tower by Tad Williams

Alfred Lord Tennyson: Ulysses

We are not now that strength which in old days moved earth and heaven; that which we are, we are; one equal temper of heroic hearts, made weak by time and fate, but strong in will to strive, to seek, to find, and not to yield.

We are not now that strength which in

old days moved earth and heaven; that

which we are, we are; one equal temper of

heroic hearts, made weak by time and

fate, but strong in will to strive, to seek,

to find, and not to yield.

Ulysses (That which we are we are)

by Alfred Lord Tennyson

Ayn Rand: Atlas Shrugged

Do not let your fire go out, spark by irreplaceable spark in the hopeless swamps of the not-quite, the not-yet, and the not-at-all. Do not let the hero in your soul perish in lonely frustration for the life you deserved and have never been able to reach. The world you desire can be won. It exists.. it is real.. it is possible.. it's yours.

Do not let your fire go out, spark by irreplaceable

spark in the hopeless swamps of the not-quite, the

not-yet, and the not-at-all. Do not let the hero in

your soul perish in lonely frustration for the life

you deserved and have never been able to reach. The

world you desire can be won. It exists.. it is real..

it is possible.. it's yours.

Atlas Shrugged by Ayn Rand

Mark Twain: The Adventures of Huckleberry Finn

Right is right, and wrong is wrong, and a body ain't got no business doing wrong when he ain't ignorant and knows better. Just because you're taught that something's right and everyone believes it's right, it don't make it right.

Right is right, and wrong is wrong, and a body

ain't got no business doing wrong when he ain't

ignorant and knows better. Just because you're

taught that something's right and everyone believes

it's right, it don't make it right.

The Adventures of Huckleberry Finn

by Mark Twain

Robert Louis Stevenson: Treasure Island

Fifteen men on the Dead Man's Chest
Yo-ho-ho, and a bottle of rum!
Drink and the devil had done for the rest
Yo-ho-ho, and a bottle of rum!

Fifteen men on the Dead Man's Chest

Yo-ho-ho, and a bottle of rum!

Drink and the devil had done for the rest

Yo-ho-ho, and a bottle of rum!

Treasure Island by Robert Louis Stevenson

Gilbert & Sullivan: Pirates of Penzance

I am the very model of a modern Major-General,
I've information vegetable, animal, and mineral,
I know the kings of England, and I quote the fights historical,
From Marathon to Waterloo, in order categorical;
I'm very well acquainted too with matters mathematical,
I understand equations, both the simple and quadratical,
About binomial theorem I'm teeming with a lot o' news---
With many cheerful facts about the square of the hypotenuse.

I am the very model of a modern Major-General,

I've information vegetable, animal, and mineral,

I know the kings of England, and I quote the

fights historical, From Marathon to Waterloo,

in order categorical; I'm very well acquainted too

with matters mathematical, I understand equations,

both the simple and quadratical, About binomial

theorem I'm teeming with a lot o' news---

With many cheerful facts about the square of the

hypotenuse.

The Pirates of Penzance by Gilbert & Sullivan

Rudyard Kipling: If

If you can keep your head when all about you
Are losing theirs and blaming it on you;
If you can trust yourself when all men doubt you,
But make allowance for their doubting too:
If you can wait and not be tired by waiting,
Or, being lied about, don't deal in lies,
Or being hated don't give way to hating,
And yet don't look too good, nor talk too wise;

If you can dream---and not make dreams your master;
If you can think---and not make thoughts your aim,
If you can meet with Triumph and Disaster
And treat those two impostors just the same:.
If you can bear to hear the truth you've spoken
Twisted by knaves to make a trap for fools,
Or watch the things you gave your life to, broken,
And stoop and build'em up with worn-out tools;

If you can make one heap of all your winnings
And risk it on one turn of pitch-and-toss,
And lose, and start again at your beginnings,
And never breathe a word about your loss:
If you can force your heart and nerve and sinew
To serve your turn long after they are gone,
And so hold on when there is nothing in you
Except the Will which says to them: "Hold on!"

If you can talk with crowds and keep your virtue,
Or walk with Kings---nor lose the common touch,
If neither foes nor loving friends can hurt you,
If all men count with you, but none too much:
If you can fill the unforgiving minute
With sixty seconds' worth of distance run,
Yours is the Earth and everything that's in it,
And---which is more---you'll be a Man, my son!

If you can keep your head when all about you

Are losing theirs and blaming it on you;

If you can trust yourself when all men doubt you

But make allowance for their doubting too:

If you can wait and not be tired by waiting,

Or, being lied about, don't deal in lies,

Or being hated don't give way to hating,

And yet don't look too good, nor talk too wise;

If you can dream---and not make dreams your

master;

If you can think---and not make thoughts your

aim,

If you can meet with Triumph and Disaster

And treat those two impostors just the same:.

If you can bear to hear the truth you've spoken

Twisted by knaves to make a trap for fools,

Or watch the things you gave your life to, broken,

And stoop and build'em up with worn-out tools;

If you can make one heap of all your winnings

And risk it on one turn of pitch-and-toss,

And lose, and start again at your beginnings,

And never breathe a word about your loss:

If you can force your heart and nerve and sinew

To serve your turn long after they are gone,

And so hold on when there is nothing in you

Except the Will which says to them: "Hold on!"

If you can talk with crowds and keep your virtue,

Or walk with Kings---nor lose the common touch,

If neither foes nor loving friends can hurt you,

If all men count with you, but none too much:

If you can fill the unforgiving minute

With sixty seconds' worth of distance run,

Yours is the Earth and everything that's in it,

And---which is more---you'll be a Man, my son!

If by Rudyard Kipling

William Ernest Henley: Invictus

Out of the night that covers me,
Black as the Pit from pole to pole,
I thank whatever gods may be
For my unconquerable soul.

In the fell clutch of circumstance
I have not winced nor cried aloud.
Under the bludgeonings of chance
My head is bloody, but unbowed.

Beyond this place of wrath and tears
Looms but the Horror of the shade,
And yet the menace of the years
Finds, and shall find, me unafraid.

It matters not how strait the gate,
How charged with punishments the scroll.
I am the master of my fate:
I am the captain of my soul.

Out of the night that covers me,

Black as the Pit from pole to pole,

I thank whatever gods may be

For my unconquerable soul.

In the fell clutch of circumstance

I have not winced nor cried aloud.

Under the bludgeonings of chance

My head is bloody, but unbowed.

Beyond this place of wrath and tears

Looms but the Horror of the shade,

And yet the menace of the years

Finds, and shall find, me unafraid.

It matters not how strait the gate,

How charged with punishments the scroll.

I am the master of my fate:

I am the captain of my soul.

Invictus by William Ernest Henley

James Joyce: A Portrait of the Artist as a Young Man

He wanted to cry quietly but not for himself:
for the words, so beautiful and sad, like music.

He wanted to cry quietly but not for himself: for

the words, so beautiful and sad, like music.

A Portrait of the Artist as a Young Man

by James Joyce

The Constitution of the United States of America

We the People of the United States, in Order to form a more perfect Union, establish Justice, insure domestic Tranquility, provide for the common defence, promote the general Welfare, and secure the Blessings of Liberty to ourselves and our Posterity, do ordain and establish this Constitution for the United States of America.

We the People of the United States, in Order to form

a more perfect Union, establish Justice, insure

domestic Tranquility, provide for the common

defence, promote the general Welfare, and secure the

Blessings of Liberty to ourselves and our Posterity,

do ordain and establish this Constitution for the

United States of America.

Jane Austen: Pride and Prejudice

I declare after all there is no enjoyment like reading! How much sooner one tires of any thing than of a book! -- When I have a house of my own, I shall be miserable if I have not an excellent library.

I declare after all there is no enjoyment like

reading! How much sooner one tires of any thing

than of a book! When I have a house of my own,

I shall be miserable if I have not an

excellent library.

Pride and Prejudice by Jane Austen

Harper Lee: To Kill a Mockingbird

I wanted you to see what real courage is, instead of getting the idea that courage is a man with a gun in his hand. It's when you know you're licked before you begin, but you begin anyway and see it through no matter what.

I wanted you to see what real courage is, instead

of getting the idea that courage is a man with a

gun in his hand. It's when you know you're licked

before you begin, but you begin anyway and see it

through no matter what.

To Kill a Mockingbird by Harper Lee

Madeleine L'Engle: A Wrinkle in Time

*I don't understand it any more than you do, but one thing
I've learned is that you don't have to understand things for
them to be.*

I don't understand it any more than you do, but

one thing I've learned is that you don't have to

understand things for them to be.

A Wrinkle in Time by Madeleine L'Engle

Mary Shelley: Frankenstein

The world to me was a secret, which I desired to discover; to her it was a vacancy, which she sought to people with imaginations of her own.

The world to me was a secret, which I desired to

discover; to her it was a vacancy, which she

sought to people with imaginations of her own.

Frankenstein by Mary Shelley

Samuel Taylor Coleridge: Kubla Khan

In Xanadu did Kubla Khan
A stately pleasure-dome decree:
Where Alph, the sacred river, ran
Through caverns measureless to man
Down to a sunless sea.
So twice five miles of fertile ground
With walls and towers were girdled round:
And there were gardens bright with sinuous rills,
Where blossomed many an incense-bearing tree;
And here were forests ancient as the hills,
Enfolding sunny spots of greenery.

In Xanadu did Kubla Khan

A stately pleasure-dome decree:

Where Alph, the sacred river, ran

Through caverns measureless to man

Down to a sunless sea.

So twice five miles of fertile ground

With walls and towers were girdled round:

And there were gardens bright with sinuous rills,

Where blossomed many an incense-bearing tree;

And here were forests ancient as the hills,

Enfolding sunny spots of greenery.

Kubla Khan by Samuel Taylor Coleridge

Shakespeare: As You Like It, Act 2 Scene 7

All the world's a stage, And all the men and women merely players; They have their exits and their entrances, And one man in his time plays many parts

All the world's a stage,

And all the men and women merely players;

They have their exits and their entrances,

And one man in his time plays many parts

As You Like It, Act 2 Scene 7, by Shakespeare

Christina Rossetti: Remember

Remember me when I am gone away,
Gone far away into the silent land;
When you can no more hold me by the hand,
Nor I half turn to go, yet turning stay.
Remember me when no more day by day
You tell me of our future that you plann'd:
Only remember me; you understand
It will be late to counsel then or pray.
Yet if you should forget me for a while
And afterwards remember, do not grieve:
For if the darkness and corruption leave
A vestige of the thoughts that once I had,
Better by far you should forget and smile
Than that you should remember and be sad.

Remember me when I am gone away,

Gone far away into the silent land;

When you can no more hold me by the hand,

Nor I half turn to go, yet turning stay.

Remember me when no more day by day

You tell me of our future that you plann'd:

Only remember me; you understand

It will be late to counsel then or pray.

Yet if you should forget me for a while

And afterwards remember, do not grieve:

For if the darkness and corruption leave

A vestige of the thoughts that once I had,

Better by far you should forget and smile

Than that you should remember and be sad.

Remember by Christina Rossetti

Oscar Wilde: The Picture of Dorian Gray

*I have grown to love secrecy. It seems to be the
one thing that can make modern life
mysterious or marvelous to us. The
commonest thing is delightful if only one
hides it.*

I have grown to love secrecy. It seems to be

the one thing that can make modern life

mysterious or marvelous to us. The commonest

thing is delightful if only one hides it.

The Picture of Dorian Gray by Oscar Wilde

Percy Shelley: Ozymandias

And on the pedestal these words appear --
'My name is Ozymandias, king of kings:
Look on my works, ye Mighty, and despair!'
Nothing beside remains. Round the decay
Of that colossal wreck, boundless and bare
The lone and level sands stretch far away.

And on the pedestal these words appear --

"My name is Ozymandias, king of kings:

Look on my works, ye Mighty, and despair!"

Nothing beside remains. Round the decay

Of that colossal wreck, boundless and bare

The lone and level sands stretch far away.

Ozymandias by Percy Shelley

J.R.R. Tolkien: The Hobbit

Far over the misty mountains cold
To dungeons deep and caverns old
We must away ere break of day
To seek the pale enchanted gold.

The dwarves of yore made mighty spells,
While hammers fell like ringing bells,
In places deep, where dark things sleep,
In hollow halls beneath the fells.

For ancient king and elvish lord,
There many a gleaming golden hoard
They shaped and wrought, and light they caught
To hide in gems on hilt of sword.

On silver necklaces they strung
The flowering stars, on crowns they hung
The dragon-fire, in twisted wire
They meshed the light of moon and sun.

Far over the misty mountains cold
To dungeons deep and caverns old
We must away, ere break of day,
To claim our long-forgotten gold.

Far over the misty mountains cold

To dungeons deep and caverns old

We must away ere break of day

To seek the pale enchanted gold.

The dwarves of yore made mighty spells,

While hammers fell like ringing bells,

In places deep, where dark things sleep,

In hollow halls beneath the fells.

For ancient king and elvish lord,

There many a gleaming golden hoard

They shaped and wrought, and light they caught

To hide in gems on hilt of sword.

On silver necklaces they strung

The flowering stars, on crowns they hung

The dragon-fire, in twisted wire

They meshed the light of moon and sun.

Far over the misty mountains cold

To dungeons deep and caverns old

We must away, ere break of day,

To claim our long-forgotten gold.

The Hobbit by J. R. R. Tolkien

Homer: The Iliad

Like the generations of leaves, the lives of mortal men. Now the wind scatters the old leaves across the earth, now the living timber bursts with the new buds and spring comes round again. And so with men: as one generation comes to life, another dies away.

Like the generations of leaves, the lives of mortal men.

Now the wind scatters the old leaves across the earth,

now the living timber bursts with the new buds

and spring comes round again. And so with men:

as one generation comes to life, another dies away.

The Iliad by Homer

70422728R10042

Made in the USA
Middletown, DE
13 April 2018